How to Draw
Arizona's
Sights and Symbols

Jennifer Quasha

The Rosen Publishing Group's
PowerKids Press™
New York

To the Circle Z Ranch in Patagonia

Published in 2002 by The Rosen Publishing Group, Inc.
29 East 21st Street, New York, NY 10010

First Edition

Book and Layout Design: Kim Sonsky
Project Editor: Jannell Khu

Illustration Credits: Laura Murawski
Photo Credits: pp. 7, 16, 22, 28 © Index Stock; p. 8 Lon Megargee, c. 1950s, courtesy of Collier Gallery, Scottsdale, Arizona; p. 9 © Arizona Capitol Museum 1982.020.002, Arizona State Library, Archives and Public Records; pp. 12, 14 © 2001 One Mile Up, Incorporated; p. 18 © Eric and David Hosking/Corbis; p. 20 © Darrell Gulin/CORBIS; p. 24 © Tom Bean/CORBIS; p. 26 © AP Photo/Matt York.

Quasha, Jennifer
        How to draw Arizona's sights and symbols / Jennifer Quasha.
            p. cm. — (A kid's guide to drawing America)
        Includes index.
        Summary: This book describes how to draw some of Arizona's sights and symbols, including the state's seal, the state's flag, the Grand Canyon, and others.
        ISBN 0-8239-6057-9
            1. Emblems, State—Arizona—Juvenile literature
2. Arizona in art—Juvenile literature
3. Drawing—Technique—Juvenile literature
(1. Emblems, State—Arizona 2. Arizona
3. Drawing—Technique) I. Title II. Series
            2001
            743'.8'09791—dc21

Manufactured in the United States of America

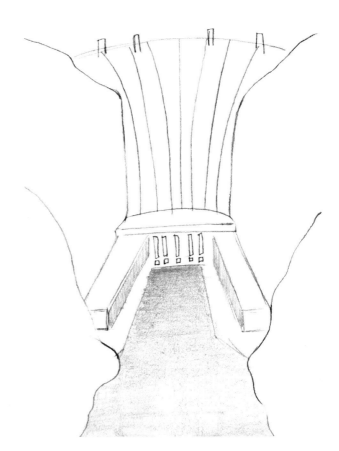

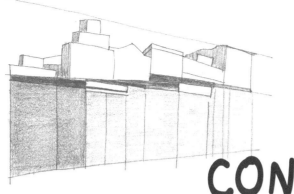

CONTENTS

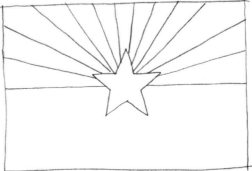

Let's Draw Arizona

Arizona is one of the fastest-growing states in the United States. It has many successful industries, including real estate, mining, transportation, and farming. It is a warm, flat state with a lot of sunshine and many wide-open spaces, such as the Sonoran Desert.

The people of Arizona are proud of their state's rich Native American history, art, and culture. The name Arizona might come from a Native American word *Ari-son*, which means "small spring." Native American heritage plays a major part in cities such as Scottsdale, Tempe, and Phoenix. Reservations, homes to many Native Americans, are scattered throughout the state. The most well known is the Hopi Indian Reservation. It has the Hopi pueblo, a village in which people have been living since prehistoric times.

Arizona has the world's largest meteor crater. It measures 1 mile (1.6 km) wide and is located near Winslow. The highest point in the state is Humphreys Peak, which is 12,633 feet (3,851 m) high.

The state of Arizona has many exciting sights and

symbols. In this book, you will learn about them and how to draw them. Begin by drawing a simple shape. From there you will add other shapes. Under every drawing, directions help explain how to do the steps. Each new step of the drawing is shown in red to help guide you. You can check out the drawing terms listed on this page. These terms also show some of the shapes and words used in this book.

You will need the following supplies to draw Arizona's sights and symbols:

- A sketch pad
- An eraser
- A number 2 pencil
- A pencil sharpener

These are some of the shapes and drawing terms you need to know to draw Arizona's sights and symbols:

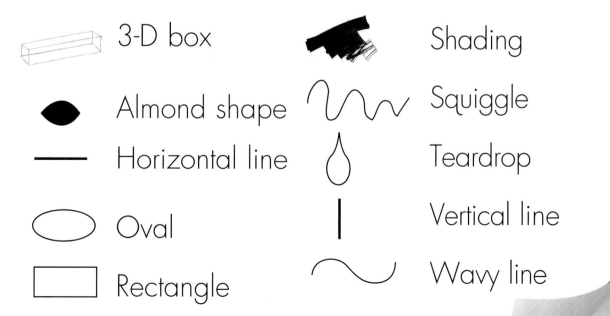

3-D box

Almond shape

Horizontal line

Oval

Rectangle

Shading

Squiggle

Teardrop

Vertical line

Wavy line

The Grand Canyon State

Arizona is called the land of sunshine because it is one of the driest states in the United States. On average Arizona's deserts get from 2 to 5 inches (5 to 13 cm) of rain each year! Arizona covers 114,006 square miles (295,274 sq km) and has a population of 4,778,300. It became a state on February 14, 1912, and was the forty-eighth state to join the United States. Phoenix is Arizona's largest city in population, and it is also the state capital. More than 1.1 million people live there. The largest Native American reservation in the world is the Navajo Reservation, which covers much of northwestern Arizona. Native American Indians called the Apache once lived in Arizona and that is why it sometimes is called the Apache State. Arizona is also the biggest copper producer in the United States. This is how it got its nickname, the Copper State. Arizona has the magnificent Grand Canyon, which is one of the Seven Natural Wonders of the World. The Grand Canyon is the reason why Arizona's official state name is the Grand Canyon State.

Sitting at an edge of a rock cliff, visitors might be able to imagine how the Grand Canyon was formed over millions of years by the Colorado River.

Artist in Arizona

Alonzo Megargee

Alonzo (Lon) Megargee was born in Philadelphia, Pennsylvania, in 1883. When he was 13 years old, Lon went to live with family in Arizona after his parents died. For several years, Lon did chores at his uncle's ranch and learned how to milk cows, fix fences, and handle horses. At age 17, he decided he wanted to look for adventure. He held many jobs, including one as a card dealer at a saloon and another as a cowboy.

In 1909, Lon left Arizona to seek an education in California. He attended the Los Angeles School of Art and Design. For six months, he focused on sketching nature in black and white. He soon realized that he liked to paint in color using oil paints so he became a colorist. A colorist is an artist who uses colors to try to show others the beauty and wonder of nature as the artist sees and feels it.

Lon returned to Arizona in 1912. A state board

hired him to paint 15 murals for the state capitol building in 1913. The oil painting shown here is one of the murals titled *San Francisco Peaks*. It shows Agassiz, Fremont, and Humphreys, the three peaks that are located near Flagstaff, Arizona. Lon observed and painted the grand landscape near the snow-capped mountains. He is also famous for the painting *Last Drop From His Stetson*, which he completed for the Stetson Hat Company. It is still copied inside Stetson hats today.

Lon Megargee died in 1961 in Cottonwood, Arizona, but his oil paintings continue to show us the beauty and majesty of Arizona's landscape.

This painting, *San Francisco Peaks*, by Lon Megargee, is at the Arizona Capitol Museum.

Map of Arizona

Map of the Continental United States

Arizona borders the U.S. states of California, Nevada, Utah, Colorado, New Mexico, and the country of Mexico on its southern border. Most of its western border follows the Colorado River. Arizona's northeastern corner is part of an area known as the Four Corners, which is the only place in the United States where the borders of four states meet. Arizona has a wide range of geographic features, including rock walls, mountain lakes, and plateaus. Arizona has the Grand Canyon National Park and the Petrified Forest National Park. It also has six national forests, including Coronado, Prescott, Tonto, and Apache-Sitgreaves. Arizona has national wildlife refuges, including Kofa and Buenos Aires.

1

Draw the angled shape as shown.

2

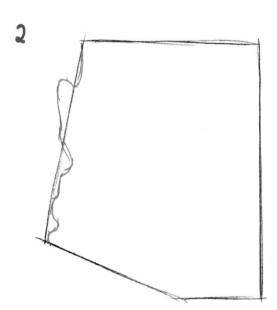

Using the map of Arizona on page 10 as a guide, draw a ragged edge on the left, or western, side of the state.

3

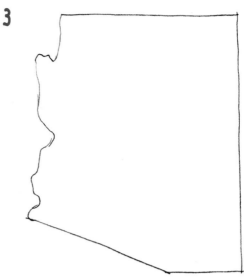

Erase the straight line on the left side. You might need to redraw parts of the ragged edge. Let's start drawing some of Arizona's sights!

4

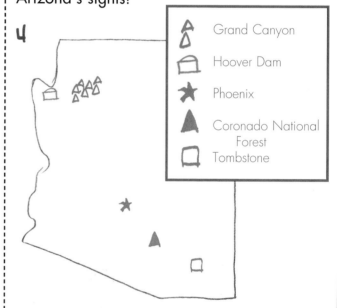

🔺	Grand Canyon
⬠	Hoover Dam
★	Phoenix
▲	Coronado National Forest
▢	Tombstone

a. Draw a five-pointed star for Phoenix, the state capital. Shade in the star.
b. Draw a triangle below and to the right of the state capital. Shade in the triangle. This is the Coronado National Forest.
c. Draw a square below and to the right of the forest. This is the town of Tombstone.
d. Draw little triangles near the top left corner of the state. This is the Grand Canyon.
e. Draw a rectangle with a semicircle on top to the left of the triangles. This is Hoover Dam.

The State Seal

Arizona's state seal was adopted in 1911. It shows many of Arizona's industries inside a shield. The sun rises behind mountains to show that Arizona is a sunny state. To the right is a reservoir and a dam. Hoover Dam is only one of the many dams that supply water to areas throughout the state. The green fields on the seal represent Arizona's many crops, including cotton. At the lower right are grazing cattle. To the left, a miner stands for the value of mining in the state. The Latin words *Ditat Deus*, at the top, are the state's motto. The words mean "God Enriches." "Great Seal of the State of Arizona" and the year 1912, when Arizona became a state, appear around the shield.

1

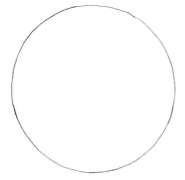

Draw a circle.

2

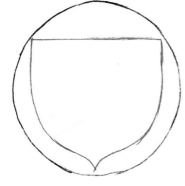

Draw the shield shape as shown.

3

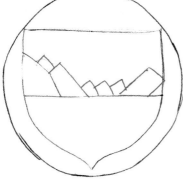

Draw a horizontal line and little triangles as shown. The triangles are mountains.

4

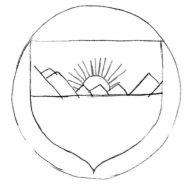

Draw a semicircle for the sun behind the mountains. Add lines to the sun for its rays.

5

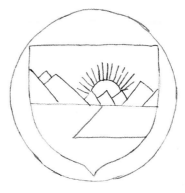

Draw an angular shape below the horizontal line as shown.

6

Draw two slanted lines and two horizontal lines. These lines are fields of crops.

7

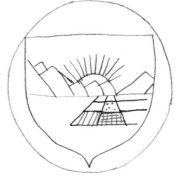

Fill in the boxes you just made with more horizontal and vertical lines and little dots as shown. Great job!

The State Flag

Arizona's state flag was created by a man named Charles W. Harris and was approved in 1917. The flag celebrates the success of the state's copper industry. In the center of the flag is a copper-colored star, representing Arizona as the greatest copper producer in the nation. The bottom half of the flag is a dark blue color. The top half of the flag has 13 rays that fan out from the center of the flag and that stretch toward the flag's top and upper corners. Six of the rays are yellow and seven are red, and the rays alternate in color. The colors blue and yellow are the state's colors, and red and yellow are the colors of the Spanish explorer Francisco Coronado and his expedition. In 1540, Coronado and the Spaniards came to Arizona after they had explored Mexico.

1

Draw a rectangle.

3

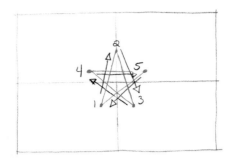

Next draw a five-pointed star in the middle, where the two lines cross. Notice the numbers that show the order in which you draw the lines.

2

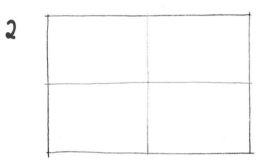

Draw one vertical line and one horizontal line that cross in the center of the rectangle.

4

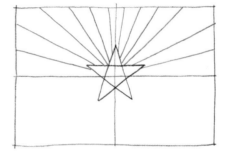

Great job! Now draw 12 lines that start from the star and go to the edges of the rectangle as shown.

5

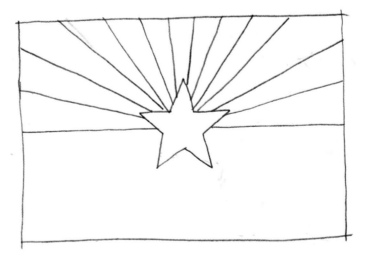

Erase the lines in the star and the vertical line below the star. Nice job! You've drawn Arizona's state flag.

The Saguaro Blossom

Arizona's state flower is the blossom that grows on the tip of the arm of the saguaro, or giant cactus. A saguaro is one of about 1,000 cacti native to North America. The saguaro can grow to 60 feet (18 m) high and can be found throughout Arizona. Its blossom was accepted as the state flower on March 16, 1931. The white saguaro flowers bloom at night in May and June every year and they have a sweet smell. The flowers' scent attracts bees and flies during these two months. In July a saguaro's blossoms turn into fruit that has red flesh. This fruit attracts doves that migrate north from Mexico. Native Americans, such as the Papagos and Pimas, make syrup from the fruit of the saguaro.

1

Begin by drawing a circle. The circle is the basic shape of the saguaro blossom.

2

Draw a smaller circle in the center of the first circle.

3

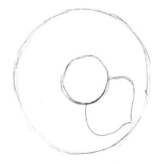

Next begin to draw the petals. Draw the curved petal shape from the center of the small circle to the line of the big circle.

4

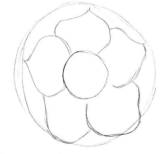

Continue drawing the petals. Notice how each petal overlaps the next one. They surround the center of the blossom. Try to draw five petals.

5

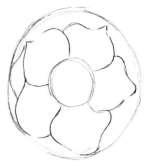

Then draw petals behind the first set of petals as shown. Don't worry about making the shapes perfect.

6

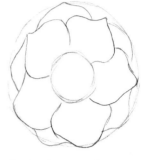

Continue to draw the petals.

7

Fill in the center of the blossom with little dashes. Draw little semicircles around the center as shown. Begin shading the petals. Shade the tiny circle in the center.

8

Continue to shade by pressing harder on your pencil. Work slowly. Gradually shade in the drawing. The areas around the center should be the darkest.

17

The Palo Verde

Arizona's state tree is the palo verde. The Spanish words *palo verde* mean "green stick." Although it was adopted as the state tree in 1954, the palo verde is not even a tree! It is not a conifer, an evergreen, a palm, or a deciduous tree. The palo verde, which is found in the desert, is a legume, or a vegetable! Palo verdes are short and thick, and they are yellow or green in color. Their yellow-gold flowers bloom in April or May. Several kinds of palo verdes, including the blue palo verde and the foothill palo verde, blossom in the southwestern United States. In the summer, pocket mice and kangaroo rats like to eat the palo verdes' brown seed pods.

1

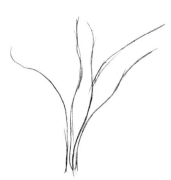

Draw four or five wavy vertical lines. These are the trunk and the main branches of the palo verde.

2

Draw lines parallel to the wavy lines to complete the trunk and main branches.

3

Add little branches by drawing tiny, curved lines as shown. Don't worry about making perfect branches. Experiment and have fun!

4

Begin shading areas on the palo verde. Turn your pencil on its side and stroke the paper gently. You can practice on the side of your drawing until you get the feel for shading.

5

Great job! Continue shading in those areas. Turn your pencil in different directions while you are shading.

6

Shade in the trunk and main branches as shown. Excellent! You have drawn a beautiful palo verde!

The Cactus Wren

In 1931, Arizona adopted the cactus wren as its state bird. The cactus wren has a black back with white spots. Its throat has the opposite coloring and is white with black spots. The cactus wren has a slightly curved beak, and each eye has a white line above it. The cactus wren is from 7 to 8 inches (18–20 cm) long from head to tail, but its tail makes up about 3 inches (8 cm) of the total length. The cactus wren builds many nests, but it only lives in one. The other nests are used as decoys to draw attention away from its real home. The nests often are built inside a saguaro. The cactus' thorns help to keep the nests safe by keeping out enemies. Cactus wrens like to eat fruit, seeds, and insects.

1

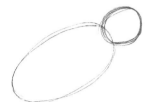

Draw an oval at an angle. This is the body of the cactus wren.

2

Draw a small circle at the top right of the oval. This is the cactus wren's head.

3

Next draw lines connecting the head to the body. Then draw in the wing by adding a curved line as shown.

4

Great job! Draw a rectangle below the back of the bird. This is the tail.

5

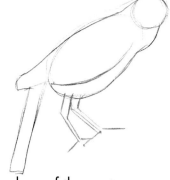

Draw the legs of the cactus wren as shown.

6

Erase any extra lines. Next draw the beak and an eye. Add the feet and a branch.

7

Begin shading the feathers. Work lightly at first. Shade the head and neck, line by line, to create a feeling of feathers.

8

Continue to shade the body, wing, legs, and feet of the cactus wren. Shade lightly and work slowly. Great job!

21

The Grand Canyon

Arizona is home to the Grand Canyon. This amazing sight is located in Grand Canyon National Park. The canyon is a jagged valley cut into Earth's surface. The Colorado River runs through the bottom of the canyon. The canyon is 277 miles (446 km) long, 4 to 18 miles (6–29 km) wide, and 1 mile (1.6 km) deep. It has been carved by erosion, or the wearing away of soil, from the flowing of the Colorado River over the last 6 million years. The river got its name from the old Spanish word *colorado*, which means "colored" or "the color red." Much of the soil in the Grand Canyon today is a reddish brown color. Visitors can ride mules down a trail through the canyon to explore this natural wonder.

1

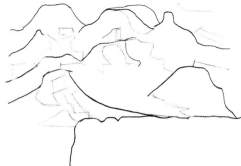

Begin by drawing two triangular shapes in the center of your paper. Then draw a sideways *L* below. These are mountains.

2

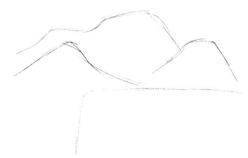

Continue to draw the basic shapes of the mountains by adding another shape as shown behind the first two triangles.

3

Add more triangles to make more mountains in the Grand Canyon.

4

Continue to draw lines in the mountains as shown. Don't worry about getting them perfect. These lines will help to guide you later when you begin shading the mountains.

5

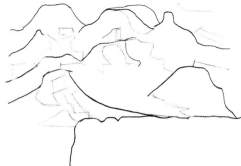

Keep adding lines to the mountains.

6

Begin to shade very lightly in the areas shown. Hold the pencil on its side and gently stroke the paper. Practice on the side of your drawing until you get the feel for shading.

7

Shade some of the areas a little darker than others, as shown. Press a little harder on your pencil as you shade these areas.

8

Finish the drawing by shading the darkest areas as pictured.

Arizona's Capitol

The Arizona state capitol building in Phoenix was built in 1899–1900. It was the Arizona Territory capitol before Arizona became a state in 1912. The dome on top of the building is made of copper, the mineral for which Arizona is most famous. Fifteen tons (14 t) of copper went into making the dome. The same amount of copper is used to make 4,800,000

pennies! On top of the dome is a wind vane with a zinc statue called *Winged Victory*. Inside the capitol, on the floor of the rotunda, is a mosaic of the Arizona state seal. The government grew too large to be housed in the building, so its offices were moved. Today part of the building houses the Arizona State Capitol Museum.

1

Begin by drawing a long rectangle. This is the base of the capitol.

2

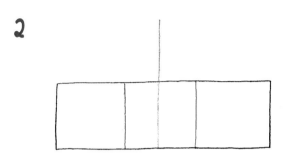

Divide the rectangle into three equal sections by drawing two vertical lines. Draw a lighter vertical line through the center rectangle. This will help to guide you through the next steps.

3

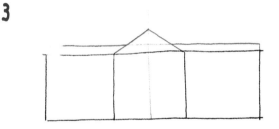

Using the guideline, draw a triangle on top of the center rectangle. Now add a horizontal line across the top of the whole rectangle. The line is lighter where it crosses the sides of the triangle.

4

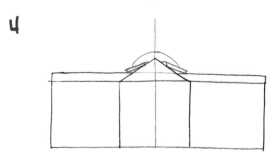

Great job! Next draw the base of the capitol dome as shown. Then draw a semicircle on top of the base.

5

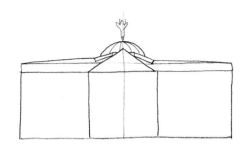

Draw a figure on top of the dome as shown. Add curved lines to the dome.

6

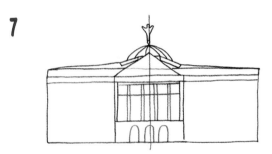

Draw four horizontal lines. One long line runs across the entire drawing and three shorter ones run in the middle rectangle.

7

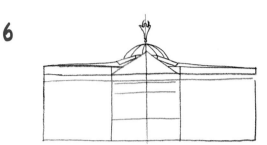

Draw eight vertical lines in the middle rectangle for the building's columns. Below, draw three upside-down *U*'s for doors.

8

You're almost done! Draw more vertical lines in the outer rectangles. These are columns. Notice how the lines extend from the bottom to the top. Erase your original guidelines.

25

The Town of Tombstone

Edward Schieffelin founded the town of Tombstone in 1877, after he discovered silver there. He named the town Tombstone because some soldiers had told him before he went to mine there that he would find only the fierce Apache and his own tombstone, meaning death. By the early 1880s, more than 10,000 people had moved to Tombstone to seek their own fortunes. The silver boom there was over, though, by the early 1900s. Tombstone's most famous event occurred on October 26, 1881. A gunfight between the Clanton gang and the Earp brothers took place at the O.K. Corral. Tombstone's gunfight and its Boot Hill Cemetery became legendary and helped give the Wild West its name.

1

To start to draw the town of Tombstone, draw three slanting horizontal lines.

2

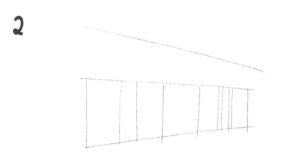

Draw 10 vertical lines to connect the bottom and the middle lines as shown.

3

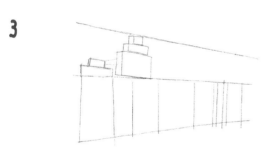

Draw little rectangles of different sizes between the top and middle lines. These are the tops of the stores in the town of Tombstone.

4

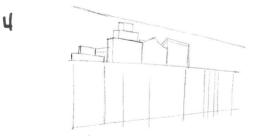

Draw more shapes between the top and the middle lines as shown.

5

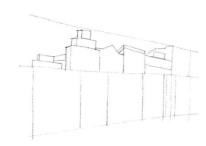

Continue to draw different shapes between the top and the middle lines.

6

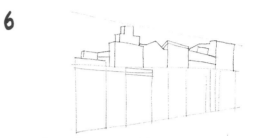

Next draw horizontal lines connecting the first four vertical lines.

7

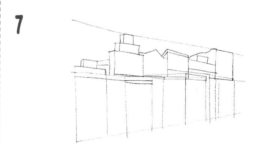

Add horizontal lines below the tops of the stores as shown.

8

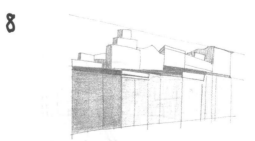

Shade in the stores as shown. Gently begin to shade in the stores. Notice how the first store is shaded much darker than the others.

Hoover Dam

The Hoover Dam sits at the southern end of Lake Mead, a human-made lake that divides part of the Arizona and Nevada borders. The 726-foot-high (221-m-high) dam controls the water flow of the Colorado River. The actual building of the dam began on June 6, 1933, and ended on May 29, 1935. Within that time, 3.25 million cubic yards (2.48 m^3) of concrete were used in building the dam. The same amount of concrete could build a highway 16 feet (5 m) wide from San Francisco to New York City! The dam was named for President Herbert Hoover. Today it is considered a national historic landmark.

1

To draw the Hoover Dam, first draw a horizontal line. Add two lines below and at a slant from the horizontal line as shown.

2

Draw an angular shape on top of the horizontal line as shown.

3

Draw two shapes to look like 3-D boxes from the two slanted lines as shown. Add another horizontal line to connect the 3-D boxes.

4

Draw two more horizontal lines. Draw the angular lines next to the 3-D boxes as shown.

5

Add squiggly lines to each side of the drawing. These are the sides of the dam.

6

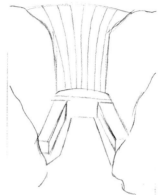

Draw vertical lines in the back shape as shown.

7

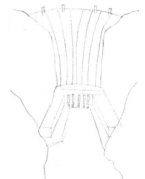

Add four tiny rectangles at the top. Draw five rectangles and squares at the bottom.

8

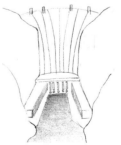

Shade the sides of the bottom rectangles. Shade in the center area. This is the Colorado River.

Arizona State Facts

Statehood	February 14, 1912, 48th state
Area	114,006 square miles (295,274 sq km)
Population	4,778,300
Capital	Phoenix, population 1,160,000
Most Populated City	Phoenix
Industries	Real estate, transportation, and mining,
Agriculture	Fruits, vegetables, cotton, and pecans
Motto	God Enriches
Nicknames	The Copper State, the Grand Canyon State, the Apache State
Fish	Apache trout
Amphibian	Treefrog
Mammal State	Ringtail
Fossil	Petrified wood
Gemstone	Turquoise
Neckwear	Bola tie
Reptile	Ridge-nosed rattlesnake
Flower	Saguaro blossom
Bird	Cactus wren
Tree	Palo verde
Song	"Arizona March Song"

Glossary

adopted (uh-DOPT-ed) To have accepted or approved something.

alternate (ALL-tur-nayt) To take turns, or to have one thing follow another.

conifer (KA-nih-fur) An evergreen tree that bears cones, such as a pine, spruce, or fir.

deciduous (deh-SIH-joo-us) A plant or tree that has leaves that fall off.

decoys (DEE-koyz) Objects used to draw attention away from something.

enriches (ihn-RICH-ez) To improve or make better by adding something.

erosion (ih-ROH-zhun) To be worn away slowly.

expedition (ek-spuh-DIH-shun) A journey made for a particular reason.

heritage (HEHR-ih-tij) The cultural traditions that are handed down from parent to child.

legendary (LEH-jen-der-ee) To be famous and important.

legume (leh-GYOOM) A vegetable, like a pea or a bean.

migrate (MY-grayt) To move from one area to another.

mineral (MIH-neh-rul) A substance, such as gold or silver, that is found in Earth and that is not a plant or animal.

mosaic (moh-ZAY-ik) A picture made by fitting together small pieces of stone, glass, or tile of different colors, and cementing them in place.

murals (MYUR-ulz) Pictures painted on a wall or ceiling.

plateaus (pla-TOHZ) Flat areas of land.

prehistoric (pree-his-TOR-ik) The time before written history.

pueblo (PWAY-bloh) A Southwest Native American village.

reservations (reh-zer-VAY-shunz) Areas of land set aside by the government for Native Americans to live on.

reservoir (REH-zuh-vwahr) A stored body of water.

rotunda (roh-TUN-duh) A round dome.

wildlife refuge (WYLD-lyf REH-fyooj) A place that gives protection to animals.

wind vane (WIHND VAYN) A tool for measuring wind direction. It spins on a rod and points in the direction from which the wind comes.

zinc (ZINGK) A grayish white metal.

Index

Web Sites

To learn more about Arizona, check out these Web sites:
www.arizonan.com
www.governor.state.az.us/kids/index.html
www.pr.state.az.us
www.state.az.us